Exponential Wealth

How to Create Sustainable Income for Life

Tim Goodwin

I'd like to dedicate this book to my girls....
to my red-hot-smoking wife, Maureen and my beautiful,
talented and wonderfully-made children Canaan, Shiloh,
& Eden

Exponential Wealth

Printed by:
90-Minute Books
302 Martinique Drive
Winter Haven, FL 33884
www.90minutebooks.com

Copyright © 2016, Tim Goodwin

Cover Design: Louie Spivak
Tortoise and Hare image: Canaan Goodwin

Published in the United States of America

Book ID: 140406-001

ISBN-13: 978-0692699256
ISBN-10: 0692699252

For more information on 90-Minute Books including finding out how you can
publish your own lead generating book, visit www.90minutebooks.com or call
(863) 318-0464

Here's What's Inside...

Acknowledgements

This book would not exist without the encouragement of my Brother from another Mother, Michael David Williams. Who believed in the message I had to share so much that he covered half the cost of getting this book done and published. Love you bro!

To my red-hot-smoking wife, Maureen – thank you for encouraging me and supporting me the whole way through, from idea to final product. And for caring so much about the beauty and design. To my kids Canaan, Shiloh and Eden who were so excited to hear their Dad was going to author a book. Especially Canaan, who asked to be my illustrator, you are such an incredibly talented girl; I cannot wait to see what your future holds.

A big hug and thank you to my good-friends Joanna Howard and Christy Trego and to my Dad, Pastor Fred Goodwin who took the time to edit this book for clarity, grammar and completeness. You guys are rock stars.

I'd also like to thank my family and friends who continued to care and ask me how the book was going, specifically Josh Goodwin & Keith Minick.

I am also grateful to my clients, some of whom are no longer with us, for inspiring me to write this message. And to other clients, mentors and authors that taught me what it means to be wealthy in a way that is also meaningful and purposeful.

Finally, to the 90minuebook.com Team. I know this book would still be an idea if it wasn't for your amazingly unique process and great team.

Thanks for reading!

You rock,

Tim

Introduction

The typical American household income (in 2015) was about $55K[1]. Assuming 2% inflation and a working career of only 40 years, the average American household will earn well over $3 million in a lifetime! Unfortunately, so few of us figure out how to save a significant amount of it and how to use it in a way that produces even more income. Instead, we spend it—and sometimes more than we earned in a given year. This results in debt and interest payments that eat away at our greatest wealth-building tool: our income. If we cannot figure out how to live on less than we make, then we will never be able to build multiple income streams and thus will never achieve the financial freedom that can lead to less stress-filled and more fulfilled lives.

Exponential wealth comes from building multiple income streams over time. One of the benefits of having exponential wealth is that it gives us better options to pursue meaningful work and meaningful experiences that we otherwise wouldn't have been able to pursue. Money can provide more options. But often a change in the way of thinking can provide that option, too, by changing the work that you are currently doing. Why are you doing the work you are doing? Is it just to earn a good income that eventually provides you a comfortable retirement, even though you don't enjoy your work?

If that's the case, I'm here to remind you, that "comfortable retirement" may not be there. We are not promised tomorrow. So why wait? Why not start

---

[1] The U.S. Census Bureau-Income and Poverty in the United States-reported real median household income of $54,462 in September 2015

dreaming up a plan to pursue something that would make you happier and might be more meaningful to you? Once you have a bigger vision and have dreamed about what that added meaning in your life is (and it's different for everyone), we can enlist a plan to make it a reality as soon as possible—not when you retire many years down the road.

At Goodwin Investment Advisory, we want to help build a framework and a step-by-step plan to get to the point where you are building wealth at an exponential level in a job you *love*. Exponential wealth is composed of multiple income streams that you've been intentionally building over time.

Wouldn't it be great if you could leave your job when you wanted to? Wouldn't it be great if you knew you were on a plan to build exponential wealth? Imagine for a moment that you had the independence or freedom to pursue whatever meaningful work or experience that you'd like. I'd say go for it! If you are like many of my clients, while you are inspired to go for it, you have questions. How can I go for my dreams, without jeopardizing my future? Clarity comes from having a framework or blueprint that shows you how to have sustainable income for life. Keep reading. This book shows you not only how you can do it, but also how I've done it, and how many of my clients and friends have done it too.

Enjoy the book!

I hope this book inspires you to be more intentional about the impact your money makes on your happiness and the wellbeing of those around you.

To Your Exponential Wealth!

Tim Goodwin

Why More People Don't Have Sustainable Income for Life After Retirement

According a recent study, 80% of Americans aren't fully confident they'll have enough money to retire[2]. They aren't confident they'll have enough income once they stop their day job. Why don't more people have sustainable income for life after retirement?

1. Culture
2. Social Security
3. Pension Plans
4. The Stock Market

Often we can get so focused on building a great income that we forget to build our net worth. We live in an income statement rich, balance sheet poor culture. It is so easy to spend all the money we make and so difficult to intentionally plan to build our assets and future income streams. In America, we generally see that there's a big group of folks who make great incomes but a much smaller group of folks that have actually saved any of that income. I think that there are a number of reasons for that.

One may be that we already know about one future income stream: Social Security. Many of us have or had parents that received income in the form of Social Security benefits. Once we start working, we

---

[2] Benefit Research Institute 2016 Retirement Confidence Survey

start to see our own Social Security benefits grow. However, we also know that the benefits of Social Security are in jeopardy. In 2033, the Social Security trust is going to run out, and if we don't fix it before then, benefits will be cut. In that situation they'd be cut down to only 77 cents on the dollar of benefits.

But good news! I'm 100% confident they will fix this, most likely right before that happens. Why do I believe this so confidently? Because they've fixed it in the past—multiple times. I'll address this in more detail later, however if you are just depending on Social Security for 100% of your future income, you are not on a good course to achieve financial peace and certainly not on the course that we recommend to achieve Exponential Wealth.

> "Social Security benefits are **not intended to be your only source of income when you retire**. On average, Social Security will replace about 40 percent of your annual pre-retirement earnings. You will need other savings, investments, pensions, or retirement accounts to make sure you have enough money to live comfortably when you retire."
>
> *Carolyn W. Colvin, Acting Commissioner*
> *Social Security Administration*

Another reason Americans may not be saving a substantial part of their income is due to an expected future Pension plan benefit. Having a Pension benefit just means that you've worked at a company, usually a very large one, for so many years, that as an added benefit, they are going to replace some of your income when you are gone with a fixed income stream. It's sort of a private version of Social Security. But many of those pension plans are being phased out. During the financial crisis of 2008, numerous pensions struggled to continue providing full benefits, especially after a bankruptcy.

Since many employees know that pension benefits are at risk, employers are more commonly giving employees their own plan to contribute to—the most popular being a 401(k) plan.

Coming back to our personal income statement versus our personal balance sheet: if we don't spend all of our income then we can add assets to our balance sheet. These employer-sponsored plans are one great way to build a future income stream (especially because they often come with a company match you can keep once you've worked there a while, once you are fully vested).

These employer-sponsored plans generally have a pre-selected, limited number of funds to invest in. Many 401(k) companies give you options to invest in retirement target date funds and asset allocated funds that give you diversification in just one fund. We highly recommend these funds unless you employ a trustworthy financial professional that will build a portfolio in your 401(k) that is customized based on your goals and appetite for risk.

Another reason most of us are not effectively building multiple income streams comes from a lack of understanding when it comes to one of my favorite things to talk about—the stock market. The stock market is always a hot topic on any news media outlet, and it's certainly a hot topic around the Keurig when people are talking about what stocks are making money, and what stocks are not.

A lot of people know, either through school or word of mouth, that the stock market is the superior performing asset class. Historically, investors could have earned average, double digit returns of 10, 11, or 12 percent annually, depending on what you invested in and for how long.

But unfortunately, our brains are just not wired to buy and hold the stocks when the stock market experiences tremendous volatility. It always has and it always will, so we have to remember (and it's very hard to do) that when the stock market tanks and the money that we once put in there is worth less than what we started with, we've reached a great opportunity to buy. It's counter-intuitive to keep buying stocks as they tank, however that's a strategy we must follow to win with the stock market.

I think that's why people, like me—Investment Advisers and other financial professionals—exist. We are here to remind folks to stick with it. If they can stick with it for decades, then those investments, when managed properly, will generate a significant and sustainable income for life. If it's built and managed really well, it could ultimately be an asset left behind for your family, your church or your alma mater. That's an impact that something like a Pension Plan or Social Security can never make. But remember, it's hard for people to stick with a buy-and-hold strategy when it comes to the stock market. It can be very frustrating, which is why I recommend you partner with a trustworthy and capable financial professional who will remind you to stay the course, especially when it's tough to do so.

Why Exponential Wealth Really Equates to Endless Freedom

What does it mean for someone to have sustainable income for life?

Ultimately, it's going to mean freedom. I've created a company of financial advisers who work less on trying to create a traditional retirement for our clients, where they are no longer working and thus put out of service[3], and instead focus more on creating freedom—where they are building financial independence and working towards a financial independence date rather than a retirement/put out of service date. We believe you obtain hope for financial independence and freedom as you create and build different investments that will become multiple income streams in the future. That, if managed well, could be sustainable for life. For me, it's not about creating one income source. It's about creating multiple sources, and we encourage our clients to have at least four.

Implementing a strategy of focusing on the potential income producing assets of your personal balance sheet could also result in income for life—income that could pay, not only as long as you live, but may continue to pay your beneficiaries as well. Here are 5 of the typical income streams we discuss with our clients and will customize a plan based on their unique situation:

1) Social Security is certainly one of those income streams that we want our clients to have for life,

---

[3] One definition of retirement is to be put of service, like retiring a baseball bat or jersey

however unless you die prematurely, you cannot leave that benefit to someone else. The best way to maximize your social security benefit is to have more options for when you begin to receive these benefits. Having other income streams you can turn on certainly provides those options. Our team uses sophisticated software that runs all your possible scenarios so we can optimize your strategy based on your goals and other income streams.

2) If you have a pension benefit as well, that's great! That will provide additional options, one of which is turning it into a stock-and-bond income stream through a lump-sum payout. That way you can leave it behind to make an impact in someone else's life and not risk a future reduction in plan benefits.

3) We encourage our clients to have income from a residential or commercial rental property that, when paid off, provides increasing income for life as rent usually goes up over time.

4) We believe it's important to continue to add value to others, even later in life. Our hope is that work continues to be meaningful, exciting and fulfilling for our clients. The best scenario would be when that work is from an income-producing hobby or some type of contract, part-time work where you are in control of the amount of time and effort you put in. We strongly encourage our clients to do *something*, the reason we like saying income-producing hobby is because hobby sounds like something fun, something that you could lose track of time doing, something that you would do just because you want to, because you enjoy it. But can you get it to actually produce income for you? If our clients can continue to earn an income of $1,000 or

$2,000 a month in retirement, it significantly increases the probability of their money outliving them, especially when we consider other income streams.

5) I've certainly saved the best for last. Building your investable assets through your 401(k) at work, Roth IRAs and other brokerage savings accounts. These are my favorite ways to build an income source due to the freedom associated with them. Once you leave a company with a 401(k) balance, it can be rolled over into an IRA Rollover to join your Roth IRAs and other brokerage savings accounts in the freedom they have. This freedom includes not being limited to what they invest in[4], and for non-retirement accounts, how much you invest and when it's taken out without penalty.

I love thinking of wealth as being defined by what is most important to you. In that case, your health, family, passion within your job, passion within your hobbies, spiritual confidence, and so on could easily lead to a sense of wealth. To be honest, I have never felt wealthier than when I'm sitting on the porch with my wife sharing a cigar and a scotch while we watch our kids play in the yard. But how we obtain financial freedom in terms of exponential wealth comes down to having multiple income streams for life.

---

[4] For the most part, Retirement/Qualified accounts are restricted from purchasing municipal investments, and your brokerage account will be limited to the investments available at the custodian you choose. Typically, you still have access to over 30,000 different choices, providing much more freedom than a 401(k), and that feels good.

No One Is Promised Tomorrow

About a year and a half ago, Joe, one of our amazing financial advisers, was celebrating with his Mom and planning for her retirement.

She was a client and a great lady who was very generous and loved by her family and co-workers. She had done a great job of saving, living on less than she made, and building extra income sources through social security and real estate. The week before she retired, her company threw her a retirement party. She retired on a Friday ready and excited to do a million things. The next day, she fell from a ladder and hit her head. After emergency surgery and months in the hospital, she never regained consciousness. Shortly before this book's publishing, she passed leaving her unable to enjoy her retirement the way she so deserved. We are not promised tomorrow so do a soul-check, right now, and ensure you love the work you do today.

Another example—early in 2015, Jim, one of my favorite clients and friend, retired from Lockheed. He and his wife Channa had planned very well for retirement. They each had a pension, debt-free primary and vacation homes, and considerable investments. After some encouragement, he retired at 59, which many would consider an early age. His wife committed to work one more year as a teacher. At that time, they planned to sell their primary home and retire to their vacation home, a farm in Illinois. Only eight months later, Channa came home to find that Jim had passed from a heart attack after his normal work-out routine. There was no history of heart issues in Jim's family; he was extremely healthy. As a matter of fact, the last conversation I had with Jim was about his home-made recipe for fermenting vegetables. Even though Jim was able to retire early, he was only able to enjoy it for a few months.

I share these stories not to scare you, but to motivate you to "retire" now, but that statement needs more explanation.

Many years ago, I read an article sharing the stories of four different individuals who, for various reasons—like selling a company or receiving a large inheritance—were able to retire early, only to find that after a few weeks of golfing and gardening full-time, they felt unfulfilled. At that point one started a business she had always wanted to try, one went to work for a nonprofit, and the others went back to jobs that they loved and found meaningful. At first, they were paid less than their previous jobs, but they felt they could afford to do this now that they had considerable investments providing extra income. The interesting thing was that their salaries began increasing over time, some up to what they had previously been paid before early retirement and some beyond. They collectively shared later how they wished they had just started their business idea or gone to work for that nonprofit before their windfalls that provided for early retirement and, later, the reasons to pursue their dreams.

This is the message I am trying to convey. Please do not work a job you do not love. Said another way, do not work a job you do not get satisfaction, purpose and meaning from. One of my favorite quotes is by Lawrence Pearsall Jacks who said, "The master in the art of living makes little distinction between his work and his play, his labor and his leisure, his mind and his body, his education and his recreation, his love and his religion. He hardly knows which is which. He simply pursues his vision of excellence at whatever he does, leaving others to decide whether he is working or playing. To him he is always doing both."

Life is simply too short and even though the examples of Suzanne and Jim are rare, they do happen. The good news about Suzanne and Jim is that they loved their jobs. What a different story it would have been if they hadn't.

Don't Let Interest Go Both Ways

There are two kinds of people, those who pay interest and those who only receive it. Sure, you can be like most Americans and pay interest on loans while also receiving interest on investments, but if you remember nothing else I write, remember my urgency in deciding to get to a place where you are only receiving interest, not paying it. The truth is, you can choose to only receive interest, because taking a loan is a choice, it's not a requirement. I didn't say there isn't pressure to take loans. There is a lot of pressure. Especially now, when it is the cultural norm to:

- Go to college, whether you can afford it or not

- Buy a house, even if you do not have a down payment

- Upgrade your car, for the safety features of course

- Fix the A/C, because how could humans survive otherwise?

- Buy it now while it's on sale, we can always pay off that credit card later

I could go on and on but I think you get my point. There are many other pressures, some real, some imagined, to acquire things and experiences we cannot afford. How can you tell whether you can afford it or not? If you do not have the cash, on hand or in the bank, you cannot afford it. And it's okay if you don't have the cash, but it's not okay to stick with the plan of living paycheck to paycheck and borrowing every time you want something.

If you want to win with money, if you want to achieve and maintain exponential and healthy wealth, you have to disconnect from the rat race of buying things you cannot afford. You must decide to stop paying someone else interest and get on a plan to get there as soon as possible.

I used to think having a high credit score was something to be proud of. That is certainly how many of us were raised and what banks are rewarding. But what are they rewarding you for? Wait for it… paying them interest. The credit scoring companies do not know how much income you make or what your net worth is. Read that again, in case you dozed off so you don't miss it. All they know is how good you are at paying other people interest. A high credit score generally means you are really good at paying other people interest. Yikes! I really don't want to be good at that.

If a person has a $200K plus income, and is worth over $1M and doesn't pay anyone else interest, their credit score is effectively zero. Maybe you are thinking, sure, if I made that kind of money, and was a millionaire, I wouldn't have to borrow either. But do not miss the lesson here. Not using debt to buy what they couldn't afford gained them wealth, usually over the course of many, many years. More on that in the chapter titled Tortoises in a World of Hares.

Paying interest on some debts, while receiving interest on others, is like doing the Tango. Sometimes it feels like a few steps forward, then all of a sudden you turn around and end up right back where you started. Sometimes the debt makes you feel good and look as pretty as that rose in your mouth. Until you realize that roses taste horrible. (Insert laugh here) Sometimes those twirls and dips take you to a peaceful and transient state. Until you come to and your stomach catches up with you and makes you want to hurl. Anyway, that's how strongly I feel about debt. I hope I'm not unclear.

If you want my recommendation, do not do it. If you already have consumer debt then build a savings account, get on a cash-flow spending plan (the key here is to update it before each pay period), and pay off your debts, smallest to largest.

Our team loves how Dave Ramsey teaches people how to do this. It's how my wife and I got out of debt and how many of my clients and friends have achieved the same. If you want more information on it, check out Financial Peace University at www.fpu.com. Our clients get fully reimbursed for the cost of the class once they've completed this course—that's how much we support it.

Tortoises in a World of Hares

You've probably heard of the ancient Greek fable credited to Aesop (a slave who probably lived around 560 years BC) called the Tortoise and the Hare. I will bet you would agree that sometimes it feels like we are living in a world of hares, everyone running around, trying to get rich quick. Everybody's trying to hit it big by winning the lottery or inventing the next big thing. The truth is that most of America's millionaires get there over time. They are the slow-and-steady-wins-the-race tortoises, making steady progress toward their goal, while hares bounce all around them, crossing lots of ground in different directions, and never getting where they really want to be.

Be the Tortoise

One mistake I see the hares constantly making is refinancing their homes frequently. I know, I used to do it all the time… until I changed my thinking. Let me illustrate, let's say you've committed to hike the Appalachian Trail, all 2,200 (3,500 km) miles of it. On average, it takes six months to hike straight through. Now imagine one and a half months into your hike you are offered a slightly lighter backpack for the rest of your journey. The catch? You will have to add an additional one and a half months to complete your journey. Said another way, you have to hike slower. Would you do it? I wouldn't, because time is of the essence. I planned to make this journey in six months when I started and got this far just fine. I do not want it to take seven and a half months total just to make it slightly easier for me to make part of the journey.

But that's what home owners do every day in America. They refinance their mortgages every time the interest rate drops so they can get a smaller payment. And if they keep on doing this, they may never pay off their mortgages. Every time they refinance, they reset the clock and start over and it's usually a 30-year period. My advice? Stick with your mortgage. Only refinance if you can refinance without adding time to your current mortgage's remaining term.

Personal note: When my eldest daughter Canaan, heard I was writing a book, she offered to be my illustrator (she was 7 at the time). How could I refuse? Plus, she is extremely talented. So here's the drawing Canaan did for my book. Thanks Scooter!

by:Canaan age7

Drawing by Canaan Goodwin

Diversified Income Game Plan

The goal of this book is to encourage you to implement a game plan for having multiple income sources in the future. The more diversified the better. You must build sustainable income separate from your stocks and bonds. Many of my retired clients do not have to distribute regularly from their stock and bonds accounts due to other sources of income. This is a good place to be as it leaves their investable assets free to grow and remain liquid in case of emergencies. It's also part of the estate they hope to leave their children, church, and/or alma mater.

Leverage Social Security

For most Americans, Social Security is still their largest income source in their retirement years. As I mentioned before, the first page of our Social Security statements currently say, "Social Security benefits are not intended to be your only source of income when you retire. On average, Social Security will replace about 40 percent of your annual pre-retirement earnings. You will need other savings, investments, pensions, or retirement accounts to make sure you have enough money to live comfortably when you retire."

Your Social Security benefits are calculated by indexing your 35 highest-paid years of income (if you are self-employed, it may be worth considering running more of your income through payroll to increase your future benefit.). If able to delay their benefits, most recipients see an increase in benefits by at least 25 percent. I recently ran the projections from one client's Social Security statement, and she would be able to increase her benefits by 37 percent if she chose to delay drawing benefits from her full retirement age until age seventy. Wow, that's a good reward for waiting a few years!

Bottom line: if you want to leverage your Social Security benefits, consider delaying benefits. If you are self-employed, consider running more of your income through salaried payroll income versus owner distributions. Talk with your financial planner so you can make an informed decision. If you do not have one, my team would love to help you maximize this benefit.

Can I Depend on Social Security?

Until recently, the first page of our Social Security statements used to say, "Without changes, in 2033 the Social Security Trust Fund will be able to pay only about 77 cents for each dollar of scheduled benefits. These estimates are based on the intermediate assumptions from the Social Security Trustees' Annual Report to the Congress." They have since removed this statement. However, in the words of Michael Kitces[5],

> "I'm not sure how realistic it is to plan for cuts. Politicians like getting re-elected. You do not get re-elected by cutting benefits for what by then may be 80,000,000 senior voters.
>
> Remember that this isn't the first time we've had a problem due to the imbalance of workers to retirees. We faced this 30 years ago as well. The shortfall was looming in 1983. We got within WEEKS of it happening, and then "fixed" it for another 50 years. That was when we began adjusting the full retirement age from 65 to 67, and making a number of other adjustments to extend it another 50 years. Given the normal political process, I would anticipate something similar. We will "fix" it sometime in the early 2030s. The math isn't hard – we know EXACTLY what to do. It's just a matter of deciding which levers to pull to

---

[5] Michael Kitces is an American financial planner, commentator, speaker, and educator. He frequently contributes to industry publications, publishes a blog and newsletter for advisors, is an editor of the Journal of Financial Planning, and is a partner of Pinnacle Advisory Group, a financial advisory firm.

make the fix, which isn't very politically appealing, until it's necessary."

Have a Paid-Off Home

Having a paid-off home won't produce income for you in retirement. However, it will reduce your budget significantly by eliminating what is usually the biggest expense—your mortgage payment. Do not get trapped in the cycle of refinancing; just stick to your plan and pay it off. Better yet, do it early. Making an extra mortgage payment each year (totaling 13 payments in a 12-month period) could reduce a 30-year mortgage loan to approximately 23 years. The most budget-friendly way to do this is to pay one-twelfth extra each month. Just make sure your mortgage company credits it as an additional principal payment and not a pre-payment. It's a good idea to stay on top of them to ensure they continue to do so.

Have a Paid-Off Rental

Imagine having strangers pay off a rental property for you, and then later having that property generate income (that generally increases over time) every month on a debt-free property. Sounds pretty good to me. Do not let being a landlord scare you. If you are not up for managing the property yourself, you can always hire a management company to find great tenants, keep them paying on time, and maintain your property.

Maintain an Income Producing Hobby

Having an income producing hobby later in life not only adds to your happiness and purpose in life, but adding another $1K per month in income can drastically improve your chances of having your money last as long as you need it. And if you enjoy making sellable items, websites like eBay, Etsy, and Amazon make it easier than ever before to earn income without even leaving your home.

One of our clients, our poster child for part-time income in retirement years, retired as an employee after a great career at IBM. She then decided to continue to provide value to IBM through a contractor relationship. This gives her the flexibility to work when she wants on the projects she wants. She typically earns $250K a year, part-time at age 70, no joke.

Having these different income sources prevents worry and stress when the stock market declines, your rental is vacant, or Social Security benefits threaten to be cut. As long as these things do not all happen at once, which is very unlikely, you will have three or more other sources of income at a time when one may be jeopardized or unavailable.

The Mindset of the Wealthy

If you ever get to meet or spend time with people who earned their wealth, you'll quickly realize they think differently from most people. They are always looking at the long game. They measure risk well and always consider the long-term impact.

They also tend to believe the best, which I think is very important. They do not look for the negative; they look for and find the positive. Any time that we have an expectation and the following behavior does not line up with that expectation, there's a gap. There's a gap between what we expected to happen and the behavior that took place. Whenever you have that gap, you can respond in one of two ways. You can either believe the best or assume the worst[6]. To illustrate, you are meeting someone for coffee, but he's running late. Your expectation was for him to be on time, but he's running late.

The natural default is to assume the worst, like "He just didn't make it a priority like I did. He isn't as on top of things as I am. He probably had something better to do, so he's not respecting my time." Then he shows up and the reality is there was a bad accident and he was stuck in traffic.

The same thing happens with stocks; they don't always behave the way we want them to. However, we must believe the best—that they will always come back, because (up to this point) they always

---

[6] Also a concept I learned from Andy Stanley who was ranked one of the top 10 most influential pastors in 2010 Survey conducted by LifeWay Research

have and they will continue to be a bigger and bigger part of a well-diversified income plan for sustainable living.

The wealthy also understand that social security and pension plans will not provide them with the financial freedom and independence that they have dreamt of. They tend to rely more on what they can save in their 401(k) and other brokerage accounts. They also understand that in order to realize a great average annual return on their stocks and bonds they must invest in a well-diversified portfolio over time.

They understand how to manage risk with this strategy as well. That during our younger years, we can have close to 100 percent of our investments in stocks, but over time, as you travel down the accumulation period of time, that risk must be reduced by bringing more bonds into play to offset the volatility of the stocks in the portfolio. As they reduce that volatility, they can begin to plan and get an idea of how much income their assets could produce and for how long.

When it comes to investing in real estate, there will be tough times when it is vacant or a deal won't go through, however I continue to observe that the very successful and wealthy individuals around me are believing the best, not just about their properties and investments, but with their relationships as well. If you do not believe the best, you are likely assuming the worst, and when it comes to investments it can often result in selling lower and buying higher. Just the opposite of how you make money. However, if you believe the best: "Hey, it's going to turn around. It's going to come back, and always has, and I'm just going to have some patience." That tends to produce much better and sometimes exponential results.

How to Prioritize Your Wealth-Building Habits

How do we prioritize? Should we pay down the house? Pay off the credit cards? Save for retirement? How do we know which to tackle first?

Dave Ramsey created what he calls the Seven Baby Steps. I like that he calls them baby steps, because that means they are approachable. They are simple to understand, but they are really not babyish. Often when I am advising people who are trying to build wealth, these Seven Baby Steps are their financial plan. They can even transcend wealth levels. Even some of my clients who are millionaires, are also trying to implement these baby steps in their lives.

However, we don't encourage the spread too thin strategy. You do not want to be like Bilbo Baggins in *The Fellowship of the Ring* when he felt "thin, sort of stretched, like butter scraped over too much bread."

As the years go by, you want to feel like you are making progress. However, if you continue to try and make progress on all your goals at once you may end up feeling like you haven't made a dent in your balance sheet. Instead, I recommend a laser-focused approach, where you are doing one thing at a time and zapping it away completely before you move on. That's how you will accomplish significant progress.

We certainly have clients walk in all the time who are paying a little bit extra on their student loans, a little bit extra on their car loans, and a little bit extra on their mortgages. They are trying to contribute to their Roth IRAs while also trying to take advantage of their company match in their 401(k).

It's like that famous Dr. Phil question, "How's that working for you?" Not too good Doc.

Those clients feel like they are getting spread too thin, and a lot of times those folks have no savings. The conversation typically goes like this: Tim: "How much money is in your savings account?" Client: "What savings account?" Tim: "Well, how much money is in your checking account?" Client: "Well, a couple thousand bucks that are intended for my bills in the next few weeks, but I don't have a savings account." Yikes!

With Dave's Seven Baby Steps, the first thing you do is build up your emergency fund. Baby Step 1 is to put $1,000 in a savings account. If you didn't have one before, open one up. The second step, Baby Step 2, is to get out of debt, everything but your primary mortgage. You do so through a debt snowball, where you pay off your smallest debt first to give yourself some confidence. It's all about human behavior: once you've seen that you've made some traction on the smaller debts, it gives you more confidence to move towards the next one, because you've already eliminated one! As you pay off each loan, you also take the minimum payment from the smaller debts and add it to your payments of your next loan—this gets that snowball effect growing, and causes you to pay off your debts at a quicker pace.

Next is Baby Step 3, after everything's paid off except the house. Here, you build up your savings account to cover three to six months of expenses. With a typical client, that can be at least $10,000, sometimes maxing out at $20,000. After that amount is set aside, generally clients want to earn more than an average savings rate at a bank on savings beyond that amount.

Baby Step 4 is to save 15 percent of your income toward retirement. For a couple, use your total household income to calculate your 15 percent. We encourage our clients to max their 401(k) contribution to get the company match first, then fund a Roth IRA, and if they still need to save more than that to get to 15 percent, invest the rest in their 401(k) to increase it above the match.

We generally encourage clients to save 15 percent of their income towards their retirement; however, at that point we can run a forecast for them to see where it could get them. If 15 percent isn't enough, we can bump it up. If 15 percent is too much, we can bump it down, but generally people are usually behind rather than ahead, so we tend to recommend increasing retirement savings. Once clients are saving 15 or 20 percent of their income, we encourage them to plan to pay off their primary mortgage so that the house is paid off sooner than the original mortgage term. You may also want to consider saving for future college expenses, if those apply. Finally, with the increased margin, you are able to do other things to build wealth, like buying rental properties or some of these other income sources that we've covered. That's generally the plan we encourage. We do not want anyone spread too thin by trying to do everything at once.

For the complete list of the Seven Baby Steps visit Dave Ramsey's website. A quick Google search should suffice or you can contact my team and we'll provide it to you.

Couple's Therapy

According to a recent survey, the leading cause of stress in a relationship stems from money fights and money problems[7].

In our financial planning practice, we frequently work with couples; and sometimes it includes Couple's Therapy. We talk about their financial plans, and occasionally find that some couples, for various reasons, have kept their assets separate— as individuals. Based on my experiences, that often leads to less than desirable results. Generally, they begin to realize, "Whenever we retire or move toward our financial independence plan, we've got to bring our finances together." When they hire us, it's certainly something we are continually talking about—bringing all assets together. Then we can discuss how much risk they want to take. It can be difficult to manage a sound financial plan for a couple with different risk levels. Bringing their assets, accounts and plan together also helps them to work towards a compromised, but agreed upon, risk level.

We believe that your money is tied to your heart, so when we begin to have these conversations about risk, we are talking more about what plans they want to make for their money and what kind of life they want us to prepare them for. It can get emotional, and it's the reason we always have tissues in our office. We are not psychologists or shrinks, but we tend to have times where it can be

---

[7] SunTrust Bank Survey 2015, reported by PR Newswire & CNBC on 2/4/15

emotional in a meeting, and we see some beautiful things happen within marriages during this time, where they begin to meet each other where they are, and that is very satisfying to be a part of. I think it's extremely important for a couple, married or not married, to have somebody else, who is close to them, involved with whatever financial goals they have.

Andy Stanley, pastor of one of the largest churches in America, taught me the idea of the Three Cs; whenever you want to change a habit – such as smoking, drinking, dieting, or setting up a budget, paying off debt, and building a retirement plan – implement the Three Cs: convicted, committed, connected. If you think of it like three legs on a stool, you need to have all three in place for the stool to stand. If any one of those is missing, the stool falls over. Most people can get convicted pretty easily. They look in the mirror; they want to lose weight. They look at their balance sheet or their net worth statement, and want to be worth more money or for me, at one point, just worth more than negative.

They might get committed to doing it, so they call Jenny Craig and they get on a plan, or they commit to going to Alcoholics Anonymous because they want to stop drinking, and maybe they start building a budget because they are committed to making the change.

However, the leg that most people miss is *connection*. It's critical when trying to change behavior to get into a group that's involved in working toward the same goal—that has incentives to get to the same place you want to go. I think that's why Jenny Craig works so well for weight loss; you get connected to a counselor. Alcoholics Anonymous works so well for getting sober and staying sober because you are continuously committed to a group that has the same goal.

Dave Ramsey's Financial Peace University works so well because you get in a class – a group, and you walk through life together, for a few months, trying to be intentional about getting out of debt over time. I've seen many couples attend who get committed to a plan to gain financial independence, and to build sustainable incomes for life. They both start envisioning a future that they want to achieve together and they get committed to making and following a plan to get there. These couples get committed to changing their behavior. They begin to track what they are spending and budget their money by giving every dollar a name before they get it.

If you can do that as a couple, you can get that accountability, that connectedness that keeps you on track toward your goal. It's very powerful when couples come in and focus on the same goal, the same future, and work to get there together. With single clients, we encourage them to lean on us a little bit more, and to have somebody else involved, whether it's a friend or a family member, who shares their goals and that they keep in touch with about what they are doing.

Intentional Generosity

S. Truett Cathy, who founded Chick-fil-A, died a billionaire in 2014. He wrote a little book called *Wealth, Is It Worth It?* In this short book, which I recommend everyone read, he basically answers the question by explaining, creating wealth is only worth it if you give it away. I think it's really an interesting concept to think about, and he's right. Because when you die with money, it's ultimately going to be given away. Some of it may go to the IRS in the form of taxes and then hopefully more of it is going to family, loved ones, maybe a church, alma mater or another non-profit that resonates with you.

But it's interesting to think about being generous before you die. I think it's very important to continue to be generous while you are in that accumulation period of your life, and to be intentional about it by choosing a percentage of your income to give away. In our office, we have observed that our clients who are intentionally generous with their money seem to be happier than the clients who are not. I've found that when you are working really hard and making money – and spending and trying to save part of it – if you can direct some of your hard-earned money to helping others in a way that you really love, you'll feel an increase in self-worth and happiness. The Science of Generosity Initiative at Notre Dame backed this up after a survey of 2,000 individuals over 5 years[8]. Those that

---

[8] As discussed in *The Paradox of Generosity: Giving We Receive, Grasping We Lose* by Christian Smith & Hilary Davidson

intentionally gave of their time and money were happier and healthier than those that didn't.

We've seen some other research about American millionaires; those who tend to be more generous with their money are actually wealthier than the ones who do not. That sounds counter-intuitive; if they are giving away their money, they should have less. My theory is that they have more of an open-handed philosophy with money. If they are giving it away, they are not holding it clenched tightly in their fist. When the money is clenched tightly in your fist, no one else can put any more money in your hand. Because this open-handed philosophy goes both ways, the people who are more generous are generally taking more risks with their money as well, and those risks may be paying off with better returns. The people that have money, hold onto it, go bury it in the dirt or stuff it in the mattress and do not take any risks to invest it, are not getting rewarded because they are not taking those risks.

Here are two proverbs that speak to this idea well: "Give freely and become more wealthy. Be stingy and lose everything." "The generous will prosper and those who refresh others will be themselves refreshed." That's Proverbs 11:24, and Proverbs 25:25.

At Goodwin Investment Advisory, our mission is to lead people to financial peace, independence, and generosity; so we focus on all three areas. They sound like they should go in that order, but they get all mixed up in the mess of life that we are all navigating through. Generally, we help people get to a point where they feel like they've got better control of their debt. We help by creating a plan so that all of their income (their greatest wealth building tool) isn't entirely committed somewhere else every month. As a result, they have income left to build wealth with. Then we help them figure out how to make that income build and grow to produce more income for them in the future.

We do not like to call it a budget. We call it a Cash Flow Intensifier™ because we feel like this name carries a clear goal with a more positive connotation. We encourage clients to complete this tool before they're paid to get them in control of their cash flow (hopefully with their spouse or with a friend). This helps them build up a small savings account and eliminate debt before working toward a financial independence plan, where they can start to build future sustainable income for life. We factor in Social Security, their stock and bond portfolio, and then hopefully we will have some plans for generating income in their later years, like contract work or an income producing hobby. Then we start looking at possibly buying a rental house, with plans of getting great tenants over time to pay off the mortgage.

Finally, we discuss different ways to be generous and ways that you can give anonymously. We can provide options where our clients are able to give away investments that they would otherwise pay heavy taxes to liquidate. Instead of that money going to Uncle Sam it would go to a non-profit of their choice.

I think most people want to be generous, but they are concerned that the money that they give may not be used appropriately, may be awarded to some individuals who are making too much money, or may not ultimately get through to the actual program or cause. We encourage our clients to use www.CharityNavigator.com, which is a watchdog site that peers into those nonprofits and scores them so you can compare and contrast them to each other.

How to Create Sustainable Income for Life

Our unique process is called the Goodwin Financial Navigation Process™. If you go to www.goodwininvestment.com and click on our process, you are going to see that the graphics resemble a sailboat, a tie-in to navigation, but you are also going to see that it's intentionally designed like an architect is still drawing, so it's on grid paper. We are constructing and building this sailboat together, in partnership with our clients. At the first stage, we talk about their financial independence plan. We talk about what kind of appetite our clients have for this kind of adventure of sailing through life and how to successfully get through this wealth accumulation period.

We assess their sails to see whether they are going to have enough; do we need to increase contributions? Do they need a better plan with their cash-flow to get them to that final destination? Then we help them continue to maintain their course, based on what risk they want and how they want to put wind in those sails. We are continually looking at their level of risk and reassessing it because markets are not static and life is not static. Life is continuously changing, so we use a tool called Dynamic Financial Planning. We are in a continual process of updating that plan so that our clients stay on course.

The second stage of our process is financial peace simplified. We take a deep look at how to keep your vessel afloat so that you do not feel like you are underwater. We want you to feel like you are floating, in a strong position and not taking on water. That's where our Cash Flow Intensifier™ comes in as a really good way for couples to sit down together and give a name to every dollar before they get it. This is more about controlling the cash flow. The "hull" truth is something that our firm discusses with our clients first about eliminating debt so they can build future income sources. Second, having an appropriately sized emergency fund, and third living on a budget that is updated every time they get paid. Then we partner with them to stay between the navigational buoys and make sure that not only are the clients regularly connected with their adviser and my firm, but they are regularly connected with each other, touching base frequently with their plan.

The next stage of our process is financial generosity simplified. We talk about how to sail well. We want our clients to work towards aligning their generous intentions with meaningful causes and charities. We use a tool that's available through the Fidelity Investment family, called Fidelity Charitable. It's one of the largest 501(c)(3)s, and is currently the largest donor advised fund in the country. We like using this tool as a way for our clients to channel their generosity. If they give money away in multiple areas every year and do so through their charitable account, they do not have to chase down all those individual tax-deductible receipts at tax time. They can just get one, so it simplifies the process for our clients.

It can be systematic, automatic, and free. You also have the option of being anonymous, so that you can avoid being added to a call list, and getting additional unwanted communication from those charities. We use the Charity Navigator tool as a way to ensure that the charities we talk about with our clients are legitimate, that they have high transparency and impact to their cause.

One of the stages of our process is the 401(k) Advantage™. Sometimes a 401(k) plan can overwhelm participants with verbiage. Leaving them with questions like, should I participate? How much? Is there a Roth bucket? What do I do about that? What investments do I choose?

We help our clients navigate all that information. Using a 401(k) correctly can act like a jib sail, which is an extra sail that's added to the main sail to provide supplemental power to the speed of a sailboat. If you chose to bring in Team GIA, it's all hands on deck to help manage that 401(k). Then you can say with confidence, "Hey, not just my brokerage accounts, but my employer-sponsored plans, too…everything is all lined up beautifully with my strategy and my Dynamic Financial Plan."

The last part of this stage is what we call the Two-Tiered College Approach™. This is for any of our clients who are thinking about helping a student go through college. We discuss how important it is for the student to be involved and to participate in his or her financial future. We encourage rewarding the behavior you want repeated. We encourage conversations about involving the student in saving for college—possibly encouraging them by matching some of their efforts for savings and/or the scholarships they are awarded.

We discuss how to choose the proper vessel. For example, 529 plans—a type of college saving plan—are a great vessel for some college expenses, but probably not for all. We recommend a second tier through an earmarked brokerage account. The last part of that Two-Tiered College Approach™ is the life jacket-ready approach, where we are making sure that we are equipping that student to be successful through college, by not getting swallowed up in debt, continuing to have savings and building a habit of living on a budget.

That's our unique process, The Goodwin Financial Navigation Process.

Anyone who is interested is encouraged to go to **www.GoodwinInvestment.com**. You can schedule a meeting with our team and begin our unique process. Or call us at the office at (678) 741-2370. We certainly have presence on Facebook and LinkedIn for folks who might want to check us out that way.

The 10 Bottom Lines

1) We are not promised tomorrow, so work at a job you love, even if you'll earn less.

2) Don't be income statement rich and balance sheet poor.

3) Stop paying interest to someone else; get out of debt ASAP.

4) Becoming wealthy with multiple income streams takes time—lots of time. Have patience.

5) Social Security isn't going to disappear, but it should only be one of many of your planned future incomes sources.

6) So long as you do it right, a stock and bond portfolio can be your fastest growing income source that can also leave behind the greatest impact for others.

7) You don't have to be a real estate mogul; find at least one great rental property and let strangers pay it off for you. You can even have someone else manage it for you.

8) Pensions are a thing of the past. If you have one, great, but remember that they are always in constant jeopardy.

9) Having a part-time job or income producing hobby is a great way to continue to add value to others during your retirement years and will add meaning and purpose to your life.

10) If you aren't intentional with your giving, you are missing an opportunity to be happier, healthier and wealthier.

Recommended Reading

The Total Money Makeover by Dave Ramsey

Wealth, Is It Worth It? by S. Truett Cathy

Thou Shall Prosper by Rabbi Daniel Lapin

Staying in Love by Andy Stanley (DVD Series)

The Three Big Questions for a Frantic Family
by Patrick Lencioni

The Millionaire Next Door by Thomas Stanley

The Millionaire Mind by Thomas Stanley

Winning the Loser's Game by Charles Ellis

You Can Retire Sooner Than You Think by
Wes Moss

About the Author

 Tim Goodwin is the President and founder of Goodwin Investment Advisory. He has worked in the financial industry since 2003 after graduating with a Finance degree from Berry College. He started Goodwin Investment Advisory in 2004, not because there weren't enough financial services companies, but because he felt like there needed to be a different one—one that acted in the best interest of the client and wasn't influenced by commissions paid by financial-product-making companies. He wanted to see more people winning with money, especially when it came to their marriage, work and retirement future.

Since 2004, he's built an incredible unique ability team of people that care deeply about their clients and are fueled by their vision of providing hope for thriving financial freedom through their mission of leading people to financial peace, independence and generosity.

Tim has been married since 2002 to his red-hot-smoking wife (his words), Maureen. They live on a small farm in north Georgia with their three beautiful daughters Canaan, Shiloh & Eden.

Tim's email is:
tgoodwin@goodwininvestment.com

Here's How to Create Sustainable Income for Life

You already know that the stock market can provide great returns, but it can also be very volatile, and wipe out a substantial amount of money in a short period of time. The confusing part is in knowing how to create a diversified wealth plan, so you are not dependent on just one source of income.

That's where we come in. We can help you diversify your income streams to create sustainable income for life.

Step 1: We meet with you to assess your unique situation and help you create your own independence plan, based on your appetite for risk and your goals.

Step 2: We work with you to help you answer the question "Will there be enough?" with confidence. We also provide insights about other sources of income you may not have considered previously.

Step 3: We then help you implement your independence plan and maintain your course, providing stability through changes in market conditions, income, and family changes.

Most people spend years working hard and have little to show for it. We can help you leverage the power of putting your money to work for you.

You can create sustainable income for life, which provides the freedom to retire and live on your own terms.

If you'd like us to help, please visit:
www.GoodwinInvestment.com to get started.

Made in the USA
Charleston, SC
12 October 2016